DATE DUE

12.95
2002

WORLD OF
PLANTS

FRANCESCA BAINES

STAMPLEY

How to use this book

Cross-references
Above some of the chapter titles, you will find a list of other chapters in the book that are related to the topic. Turn to these pages to find out more about each subject.

See for yourself
See-for-yourself bubbles give you the chance to test out some of the ideas in this book. They explain what you will need and what you have to do to see if an idea really works.

Quiz corner
In the quiz corner, you will find a list of questions. The answers to the quiz questions are somewhere in the same chapter. Try to answer all the questions about each subject.

Chatterboxes
Chatterboxes give you interesting facts about other things that are related to the subject.

Glossary
Difficult words are explained in the glossary on page 31. These words are in **bold** type in the book. Look them up in the glossary to find out what they mean.

Index
The index is on page 32. It is a list of important words mentioned in the book, with page numbers next to the entries. If you want to read about a subject, look it up in the index, then turn to the page number given.

Contents

All Kinds of Plants

A tall oak tree, a spiky cactus, and a small daisy may look completely different from each other, but they are all plants. Almost every plant has a **stem**, **roots**, leaves, and flowers. Each part helps the plant grow or make new plants.

The key to life
We cannot live without plants. We eat them every day and make lots of useful things from them, including furniture and medicine. The paper in this book was once part of a tree. More importantly, plants release oxygen, a gas that is part of the air we breathe. Without oxygen, every living creature would die.

▲ Plants provide us with an amazing variety of fruits and vegetables. We eat **seeds**, roots, leaves, flowers, and even bark.

Plants everywhere
Plants grow in almost every corner of the world. The most important things that make a plant grow are sunlight and water. In some places these are hard to find. In hot, dry deserts, it may rain just once a year, so desert plants survive by collecting and storing water. On the rain forest floor, there is a lot of water but little sunlight, so rain forest plants find special ways of reaching the light.

◀ Animals depend on plants, too. Giraffes use their long necks to feed on high leaves.

4

▲ Plants can live in cold, hot, wet, or windy places. These plants are growing on a cold hillside.

Quiz Corner

● Name some of the plants that you see every day.

● Why do people and animals need plants to survive?

● What are the most important things that make a plant grow?

Look at: Flowers, page 12; Woodland, page 16

Seeds

A **seed** is the part of a plant from which new plants grow. Seeds come in all shapes and sizes. A seed the size of your fingernail can grow into a huge tree. Pits, pips, peas, nuts, and grains of rice are all seeds. Some seeds are so tiny that you can hold over one million of them in the palm of your hand.

Sowing seeds

A plant needs to scatter its seeds so that they will find room to grow. Plants do this in different ways. Dandelion seeds have hairs that work like parachutes so that the wind will blow them away from the parent plant. Many seeds have hooks, or burrs, that stick to animals' coats and are carried away.

▲ When the seeds of the milkweed are ripe, the seed coat, or pod, explodes and the seeds shoot into the air like rockets.

▼ This is how a sunflower seed grows and flowers. You could plant your own seeds.

In spring, plant your seed in a sunny place about half an inch deep. Water it every day.

*Soon, food in the seed will make **shoots** and leaves appear above the ground.*

In summer, the plant will begin to flower. Remember to keep watering it.

6

The middle of the flower is made up of hundreds of seeds.

SEE FOR YOURSELF

See how hooks, or burrs, stick to fur and clothes. On a dry day, put an old, thick sock over one of your shoes and walk through a meadow. Take off the sock and see how many seeds with burrs are stuck to it.

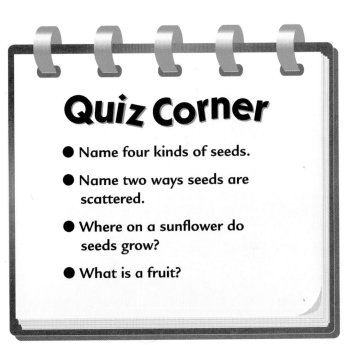

Birds eat some of the seeds.

*The **stem** twists so that the flower always faces the sun.*

Tasty protection

A fruit is a case that protects seeds. Many fruits have juicy flesh. They taste good, so animals eat them and scatter the seeds in their droppings. When the seeds are not ready to grow, the fruit tastes sour and the animals will not eat it. When the seeds are ready, the fruit tastes sweet.

seeds

A sunflower can grow over 12 feet tall. As the flower dies, cut off its head, scrape out the seeds, and plant them the following spring.

Quiz Corner

- Name four kinds of seeds.
- Name two ways seeds are scattered.
- Where on a sunflower do seeds grow?
- What is a fruit?

Look at: Desert, page 22; Water Plants, page 24; Food Plants, page 26

Roots and Stems

The **roots**, leaves, and flowers of a plant are all joined together by a **stem**. Food and water travel up and down the stem to reach all parts of the plant. While the stem pushes upward toward the light, roots at the bottom of the stem grow down into the ground, searching for **nutrients** and water.

Parts of a plant
Plants may look different from each other, but they all have the same basic parts.

Leaves and flowers .... *grow from* **buds** *on the stem.*

Plant stems usually .... *grow thicker as the plant grows taller.*

Roots hold the .... *plant firmly in the ground.*

Holding tight
Roots help to keep plants in place. In cold mountain areas, there are strong winds, and there is often little soil. Plants do not blow away because their strong roots grip the rocky cracks, where they make their homes.

◀ Plants can grow in cracks in a wall. Strong roots push into tiny gaps to hold the plants in place.

8

Big and small stems

The size of a plant's stem depends on how many leaves and branches the plant has to support. A tree's stem is called a trunk. It must be strong enough to hold up long branches full of leaves and, sometimes, fruit. Small plants have thin stems that bend and spring back in the wind or when animals step on them.

▶ The baobab tree grows in dry areas. When it rains, the tree stores water in its trunk for the long, dry months ahead.

CHATTERBOX

Grapevines have found a way to help hold up their leaves and flowers. As the stems grow, they twist and turn around frames or plants, using them for support.

Quiz Corner

- What do roots do?
- What grow from buds?
- Where does the baobab tree store water?
- How do grapevines hold up their leaves and flowers?

Look at: Trees, page 14; Woodland, page 16

Leaves

Plants are special because they do not have to look for food. A plant draws up **nutrients** from the soil through its **roots** and uses these nutrients to make food in its leaves. The leaves take in sunlight, which gives them the power to make food.

Making food

A green **substance** in leaves, called chlorophyll, collects the sun's **energy**. This energy is used to make food by mixing together water from the soil and a gas from the air called carbon dioxide. This process is called photosynthesis.

Carbon dioxide and .... sunlight go into the leaf.

Water travels up the .... stem into the leaf.

Wind and water

Leaves help plants cope with harsh conditions. In dry areas, plants have thick leaves, or leaves with rolled-up edges, to help store water. In hot, wet areas, many plants have waxy leaves so that water runs off them and they do not rot. Often, plants in windy places have feathery leaves. The wind blows through the leaves without tearing them.

10

◀ Many animals get energy from leaves. Each day, a giant panda will eat 90 lb of bamboo leaves and **shoots**.

SEE FOR YOURSELF

As plants make food, their leaves release moisture into the air. Put a plant inside a plastic bag and seal it. Soon you will see drops of water inside the bag.

Ferns and fronds

Ferns have small, fine leaves called fronds, which grow from curled-up **buds**. Ferns do not have flowers, so they cannot make **seeds**. They make new plants by releasing tiny **spores**, which are usually on the underside of the fronds. Spores are so light that they are carried away to new ground by the slightest wind.

◀ Ferns prefer to live near the ground, where it is damp and shady.

Quiz Corner

- Which gas do plants use to make food?
- Why do some leaves have waxy coats?
- What does the giant panda eat?
- How do ferns make new plants?

Look at: Seeds, page 6; Rain Forest, page 18

Flowers

Flowers are the most colorful parts of a plant. They often smell sweet, too. Flowers start to make **seeds** when tiny grains called **pollen** move from one flower to another. This is called **pollination**. Flowers need help from insects or the wind to do this.

Insect pollination

Insects enjoy feeding on **nectar**, which is a sweet-smelling juice made by flowers. When an insect lands on a flower to feed, its body is brushed with pollen. The insect flies to another flower, where the pollen sticks to part of the flower called the **stigma**. Then the flower can begin to make seeds.

▶ There are many different types of flowers of all shapes, sizes, and colors. They all make seeds in similar ways.

*The beginning of a flower or leaf is called a **bud**. This bud will grow into an evening primrose.*

*Pollen is made at the end of short stalks called **stamens**.*

Pollen from another plant lands on the stigma.

CHATTERBOX

People all over the world love the colors and smells of flowers. Flowers make good presents, and some people wear them for celebrations.

Bees are important pollinators. Every day, they visit hundreds of flowers, such as poppies.

12

Wind power

Insect-pollinated flowers have brightly colored petals and strong smells to attract insects. Grasses do not need special colors or scents. They rely on the wind for pollination. The pollen is so light that the wind blows it off the flower and carries it a long way. Some of the pollen lands on the stigmas of other grass flowers.

Wind-pollinated flowers, such as grasses, do not have petals. The wind easily blows the pollen away. ....

Quiz Corner

- What do insects carry from flower to flower?
- What is the name of the sweet juice made by flowers?
- Name a plant that uses the wind for pollination.

Meadow clary flowers have landing places for insects to feed from. ....

Insects land on the open flowers of daisies.

Look at: Woodland, page 16; Useful Plants, page 28

Trees

Trees are the biggest plants of all. They have strong **roots** that anchor them to the ground. Their thick, woody trunks allow them to grow high above other plants in search of light. Trees live longer than anything else on Earth. The oldest trees are over 5,000 years old!

Food store

A liquid called **sap** flows through the trunk of a tree. Sap is full of food made by the leaves and **nutrients** collected by the roots. The sap is protected by a layer of bark around the trunk.

▲ Giant redwood trees are among the largest trees in the world. They can grow as tall as a 12-story building.

▲ Most of the fruits we eat, such as oranges, grow on trees.

Falling leaves

There are two main types of trees: **deciduous** and **evergreen**. Each autumn, a deciduous tree loses all its leaves. In spring, the leaves grow again. An evergreen tree loses a small number of leaves every day. At the same time, new leaves grow, so the tree always looks green.

CHATTERBOX

You can tell the age of a dead tree by looking at its stump and counting the number of rings. There is a ring for each year of growth. A wide ring means the tree grew a lot during that year.

These conifers are tough evergreen trees that can survive cold and icy winters.

Quiz Corner

- How old are the oldest trees?
- What is the liquid inside a tree trunk called?
- What is the difference between deciduous and evergreen trees?
- How can you tell the age of a dead tree?

Woodland

Large areas of land that are full of trees and other plants are called woods or forests. In parts of the world such as northern Europe and North America, the weather changes during the year from a warm summer to a cold winter. Woodland plants there have to cope with the changing seasons.

▼ This is how a **deciduous** tree grows during a year. You can see how the tree, and plants that grow near it, change with each season.

CHATTERBOX

At Christmastime, some people decorate **evergreen** trees inside their homes. This tradition probably began in Germany. Christmas trees were introduced to the United States in the early 1800's by German settlers in Pennsylvania.

*In spring, young leaves on the tree grow from **buds**. Sunlight reaches ground plants so that they flower.*

In summer, the leaves are fully grown. Few plants grow in the shade of the tree because there is not enough sunlight.

*In autumn, it is cold and there is not much sunlight. The tree stops growing and drops its leaves to save **energy**.*

Animals and seeds

Many animals live in woods and forests. There are lots of **seeds** and leaves for them to eat. Many unripe seeds are protected against hungry animals. Horse chestnut seeds, called conkers, stay inside spiky fruits until they are ready to grow into trees.

Lost food

Squirrels are useful animals because they store nuts in the ground to eat in winter. They forget where they are buried, so the seeds often grow into new trees.

During winter, the tree grows buds. When spring arrives, new leaves and flowers grow from these buds.

▲ In autumn, fallen leaves rot to make a rich soil for new plants. Insects and worms also feed on the soil.

Quiz Corner

- Why is it difficult for small plants to grow in a forest during summer?
- Why are squirrels useful forest animals?
- What happens to leaves that fall from trees in autumn?

Look at: Leaves, page 10; Flowers, page 12

Rain Forest

Rain forests are warm, wet places that are tightly packed with tall trees, leafy plants, and colorful fruits and flowers. There are so many plants there that it is a struggle for all of them to find space and sunlight. Plants grow quickly because it is warm and there is plenty of rain.

Three layers

A rain forest is similar to a three-story building. Each story has its own plants and animals. The forest floor is dark and damp. **Mosses** and ferns are often the only plants that grow there. The middle layer is called the understory. There, plants have large leaves to collect as much light as possible. The top layer is called the canopy. Many animals live there, feeding on leaves, flowers, fruits, and **seeds**.

▼ Leaf-cutter ants cut leaves from the canopy and take them to their underground nests.

▲ Birds feed on the **nectar** of heliconia flowers, **pollinating** the flowers at the same time.

The ants use their powerful jaws to cut pieces of leaves from plants.

*Vines grow around plant **stems** to reach the canopy.*

Many orchids grow high up where pollinating creatures live.

▼ On this rain forest floor, green mosses cover most rocks and tree trunks.

The titan arum is a huge flowering spike. It grows in the rain forests of Indonesia. It flowers for only a few days, so it has a strong smell to attract insect pollinators as quickly as possible.

Quiz Corner

● What are the three layers of the rain forest called?

● Why do some rain forest plants have large leaves?

● Where do leaf-cutter ants make their nests?

19

Look at: Flowers, page 12

Grassland

A large, open area of land where mainly grasses grow is called grassland. Grasses are tough plants that can grow back after being eaten by animals. New leaves grow from the bottom of the plant, not the top, where they do on trees. Animals eat the tops of leaves, while new leaves grow lower down the plant.

Wet and dry

Wet areas of grassland are called meadows. Many different plants grow there because there is plenty of rain and few trees to block out the sunlight. Most meadow plants have bendy **stems** and strong **roots** so that they can survive windy weather.

▲ In spring, this American meadow becomes a colorful carpet of flowers.

Savanna

The warmest and driest grassland is called savanna. There are large areas of savanna in Africa. Many different kinds of grass-eating animals, such as zebras and wildebeest, roam on the savanna looking for fresh grass **shoots** to eat.

◀ In the African savanna, the lion hides in the tall grass, watching for **prey**.

20

Prairies and pampas

The prairies of North America and the pampas of South America are areas of cool grassland. The prairie soil is full of **nutrients** and people grow crops there. On the pampas, grass can grow up to ten feet tall—taller than two children, one on top of the other.

Cattlemen, called gauchos, look after herds of cattle.

Pampas grass flowers are tall and feathery.

▲ The pampas stretch across South America. Cattle feed on the grass there.

Quiz Corner

- Where in the world would you find a savanna?
- Name three animals that live on grassland.
- What is the grassland in South America called?

21

Desert

All plants need water to live, but some can survive with only a tiny amount. In the desert, it may rain just once a year, so plants have found ways to gather as much water as possible and store it for many months. When rain falls, many desert plants burst into flower and brighten up the dry and dusty landscape.

The clever cactus

Cacti are perfect desert plants. They have long **roots** that spread out just below the surface to collect as much rain as possible. They store water in their **stems**. Cacti protect their watery stems from thirsty animals by growing sharp spines.

▶ In the deserts of California, many plants find a home on the dry and rocky land.

Prickly pears have pads of small protective spines.

Room to grow

When there is no rain, cactus stems become thinner. These pictures show a cactus stem cut crosswise.

After rain, the stem collects water and is full of juicy flesh.

As the cactus uses up the water, its stem shrinks.

The roots of the Joshua tree search deep underground for water.

Desert oases

In parts of the desert, there are wet areas, called oases, where many plants grow, especially palm trees. People and animals depend on oases for food and water. At an oasis, water rises from below the desert. The water has flowed underground from far away, where there has been plenty of rain.

◀ At this oasis in Algeria, North Africa, fruits grow on the palm trees. People take water from a deep well near the house.

The saguaro is the tallest cactus in the world. It can grow as tall as a house. ....

CHATTERBOX

Small animals can dig holes in the soft flesh of cacti. Owls and woodpeckers often make their nests in these holes to keep their young in the shade.

Quiz Corner

- Where does a cactus store water?
- What is an oasis?
- Which animals sometimes make their homes in cacti stems?

Look at: Roots and Stems, page 8

Water Plants

Plants grow in the water as well as on land. Many seaweeds and small water plants float freely in the water, while others fasten themselves to the seabed or the mud at the bottom of a pond or lake. Along the water's edge, plants grow with their **roots** and **stems** underwater.

▲ A mangrove tree has special roots that support the tree in the soft mud along the riverbank.

▲ Sea otters sleep in the water. They wrap up in seaweed attached to the seabed so that they do not float away.

Flowerless plants

Most plants that live under the sea belong to a group of plants called algae. These plants do not grow flowers. Some of them can be seen only with a microscope. Others, such as the giant kelp seaweed, can grow longer than seven trucks parked end to end.

CHATTERBOX

In boggy areas, the soil contains few **nutrients**. The Venus flytrap, which grows along the east coast of the U.S., catches insects for food. It has leaves with toothlike points along the edge. When an insect lands inside the leaf to eat the **nectar**, the leaves shut, trapping the insect inside.

Holding fast

The roots of the water lily are fixed in the mud at the bottom of a pond. The leaves grow until they reach the surface. There, the leaves can gather sunlight to make their food. The Amazonian water lily has leaves that are large and strong enough for a child to stand on.

Quiz Corner

- Which animal wraps itself in seaweed before it goes to sleep?
- Name a plant from the algae plant group.
- Why do some plants eat insects?
- Where do water lilies fix their roots?

▲ All plants need sunlight to grow. The water lily leaves block out the light so that few other plants grow under the water.

Look at: All kinds of Plants, page 4; Trees, page 14

Food Plants

Almost everything we eat is a plant or depends on plants. Bread, fruit, sugar, coffee, and chocolate are all foods that come from plants. Grass and other plants provide food for sheep and cows, which give us meat, milk, and cheese.

SEE FOR YOURSELF

Write down everything that you ate yesterday. How many plants did you eat? Try to find out where in the world they grew. Think carefully—foods such as bread and pasta are made from a grass called wheat.

◀ We eat all parts of plants. Carrots and parsnips are **roots**, oranges and pineapples are fruits, and cashews are **seeds**.

leek

...... potato

.... celery

.... onion

coconut

cashew nut

banana

parsnip

carrot

pineapple ....

orange ....

tangerine ....

.... apple

sunflower seeds ....

▶ In Asia, farmers grow rice in fields called paddies. The farmers flood the fields with water to help the rice grow.

Important grasses

The world's three most important food plants are all grasses: wheat, rice, and corn. These plants are called cereals, and their seeds are called grains. People grind grains of wheat and corn to make flour, which is used to make bread and cakes.

Helping plants grow

Fruits and vegetables need warmth to grow. In places with cold winters, such as northern Europe, farmers grow plants in heated greenhouses. Inside a greenhouse, it feels like summer to the plants, so they produce fruit and vegetables all year round.

Quiz Corner

● Name four fruits.

● How do people grow rice?

● What are the world's three most important food plants?

● How can farmers make plants produce fruit in the winter?

27

Look at: All Kinds of Plants, page 4; Trees, page 14

Useful Plants

Plants provide us with so many useful things that it is impossible to imagine our lives without them. Every day we use things made from plants, such as paper, cotton, perfume, soap, and furniture. Even the toothpaste you use may be flavored with the mint plant.

Wearing plants
Look at the clothes you are wearing. Some may be made of cotton, which comes from plants. Are you wearing shoes with rubber soles? Rubber comes from trees. When the bark of a rubber tree is cut, thin rubber flows out. Straw is dry grass and is used to make hats.

▶ All of these things have been made from wood, rubber, cotton, straw, paper, or other plant materials.

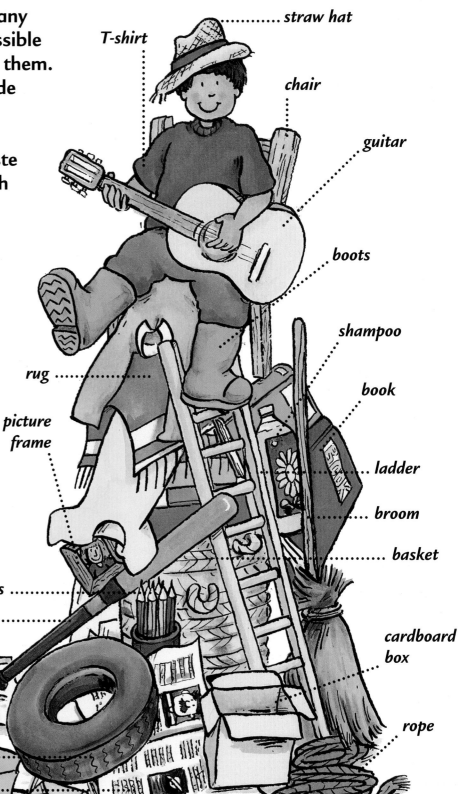

straw hat

T-shirt

chair

guitar

boots

shampoo

book

rug

picture frame

ladder

broom

basket

pencils

baseball bat

cardboard box

medicine

rope

tire

newspaper

Tree farms

Wood comes from the trunks of trees. It is strong but can be shaped easily to make many things, from boats to musical instruments. Most wood is grown on tree farms, or plantations. Once trees are cut down for wood, people replace them with new tree plants.

▼ This huge truck carries logs of wood from forests to factories.

▲ Paper is made from wood that has been soaked and mashed up. This man is making spectacular kites from huge sheets of paper.

Medicines

For hundreds of years, people have used plants to make medicines. Headache tablets were once made from the bark of the willow tree. Plants are still being discovered. Scientists hope that they will provide us with new medicines in the future.

Saving plants

Places where plants grow, from forest to grassland, are under threat from people building roads and houses or planting crops for food. Animals, as well as plants, are losing their homes. We need to protect these areas so that plants and the animals that depend on them, including humans, do not die out.

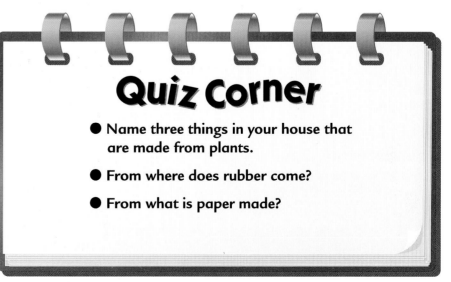

Quiz Corner

● Name three things in your house that are made from plants.

● From where does rubber come?

● From what is paper made?

Amazing Facts

● About 400 million years ago, the first land plants grew. They were simple **stems** without leaves, flowers, or **seeds**.

☆ *In 1954, a 10,000-year-old lupine seed was found in Canada, buried in frozen ground. Scientists planted the seed and it flowered. Today, scientists store seeds in freezers so that rare plants can be grown in the future.*

● The **sap** of the sugar maple tree is delicious. It is collected and boiled until it becomes a sweet, sticky syrup called maple syrup.

☆ *The flowers of the fig plant are hidden away inside the fruits. A special wasp lives most of its life inside the fig fruit and* **pollinates** *the flower.*

● The bee orchid has a very clever way of attracting male bees to pollinate it. The flower looks just like a female bee!

☆ *Some plants wear sunscreens. Sage and lavender both produce smelly oils to protect themselves from the sun.*

● The world's largest seed is a huge nut called the coco-de-mer, which grows in the Seychelles. It looks like two coconuts joined together and can weigh more than three watermelons!

☆ *Banksias are evergreens that grow in Australia where there are often bushfires. The tough fruits of these plants survive the fires and release their seeds only after the fires have died down.*

● In Venezuela, people collect and drink the sap of a type of fig tree. The tree's sap looks and tastes just like cow's milk.

☆ *Over 900 different flowers manage to survive in the Arctic. Winter temperatures are freezing, but in summer the top layer of soil becomes soft and plants begin to grow.*

Glossary

bud A small swelling on a plant that grows into a flower or a leaf.

deciduous A tree that loses all of its leaves each autumn.

energy The power to do things. Plants need energy to make their food.

evergreen A tree that keeps most of its leaves all year round.

moss A soft green plant that grows on damp soil, wood, or stone.

nectar A sweet liquid made by flowers. Nectar attracts insects for **pollination**.

nutrients Substances that help plants and animals grow.

pollen A powder made by plants. It is found at the end of the **stamens**, inside the flower.

pollination When **pollen** of one plant lands on the **stigma** of another plant so that the plant can make **seeds**.

prey The creatures that an animal hunts and eats.

roots Parts of a plant that grow underground. Roots take up water and **nutrients** from the soil.

sap The watery liquid inside plant **stems** and tree trunks.

seed Part of a plant from which new plants can grow.

shoot A new part of a growing plant. Plant shoots appear above the ground.

spore Part of a nonflowering plant that helps it to produce new plants.

stamens Short stalks inside a flower. **Pollen** is found at the end of the stamens.

stem The long, central part of a plant that supports the leaves and flowers.

stigma Part of a flower that receives **pollen** during **pollination**.

substance The material from which something is made.

31

Index

A
algae 24, 25

B
bamboo leaves 11
bees 12
buds 8, 11, 12, 16, 17

C
cacti 4, 22, 23
cattle 21
conifers 15, 16
conkers 17
corn 27
cotton 28

D
desert 4, 20-21

F
ferns 11, 18
figs 30
flowers 4, 12-13
  banksia 30
  daisy 4, 13
  dandelion 6
  heliconia 18
  lupine 30
  meadow clary 13
  orchid 18, 30
  poppies 12
  sunflower 6, 7, 26
  titan arum 19
  Venus flytrap 24
  water lily 25
fruit 4, 7, 14, 26, 27, 30

G
grapevines 9
grass 13, 20-21, 26, 27

I
insects 12, 13, 17, 30

L
leaf-cutter ants 18
lions 20

M
meadows 20
milkweed 6
mosses 18, 19

N
nectar 12, 18, 24
nuts 6, 26

O
oases 23
otters 24
owls 23

P
pampas 21
paper 29
photosynthesis 10
pollen 12
pollination 12, 13, 18
prairies 21
prickly pears 22

R
rain forests 4, 18-19
rice 6, 27
roots 8-9, 10, 14, 20, 24, 25, 26
rubber 28

S
saguaro 23
sap 14, 30
savanna 20
seaweed 24
seeds 4, 6-7, 11, 17, 18, 26, 30
spores 11
squirrels 17
straw 28

T
trees 4, 14-15, 29
  baobab 9
  Joshua 22
  mangrove 24
  oak 4
  palm 23, 30
  redwood 14

V
vegetables 4, 26, 27

W
wheat 27
wildebeest 20
wood 4, 28, 29
woodpeckers 23

Z
zebras 20

Published in the USA by
C.D. Stampley Enterprises, Inc.,
Charlotte, NC, USA.
Created by Two-Can Publishing Ltd.,
London. English language edition
© Two-Can Publishing Ltd., 1997

Managing Editor: Robert Sved
Art Director: Carole Orbell
Senior Designer: Gareth Dobson
Picture research: Laura Cartwright
Consultant: Gail Bromley
Artwork: Gill Platt, Amelia Rosato,
Teri Gower, Mel Pickering, Peter Bull
Production: Adam Wilde
Additional research: Inga Phipps

ISBN: 1-58087-003-1

Photographic credits: front cover:
Oxford Scientific Films; p. 4(t): Tony
Stone, (b): Robert Harding; p. 5: Planet
Earth Pictures; p. 6: Frank Lane Picture
Agency; p. 7: Zefa; p. 8: Bruce Coleman
Ltd; p. 9: Planet Earth Pictures; p. 10:
Robert Harding; p. 11: Tony Stone;
p. 14(r): Planet Earth Pictures, (l):
Robert Harding; pp. 15/17: Tony Stone;
p. 18: Michael & Patricia Fogden/BBC
Natural History Unit; p. 19: Robert
Harding; p. 20(t): Tony Stone, (b):
Robert Harding; p. 23: Tony Stone;
p. 24(r&l): Bruce Coleman Ltd; p. 25:
Robert Harding; p. 27: Tony Stone;
p. 29(r): Britstock-IFA, (l): Tony Stone.